About the Illustrator:

Kelsey DeLange is a Michigan-based illustrator and creator of the art and lifestyle brand Best Wishes. Kelsey specializes in blending natural and celestial imagery with powerful hand-lettered messages to create whimsical, uplifting illustrations that inspire you to turn inward, practice mindful living, and celebrate your divine power. Her work has been featured by various outlets such as *Buzzfeed*, *HelloGiggles*, *ModCloth*, and by Martha Stewart, to name a few.